JOURNEY JOHNSON

NECESSARY JOURNEY

NECESSARY JOURNEY

CONTENTS

Dedication
viii

– Necessary Journey
2

– Window Revelations
3

– The End of Patience
10

– They Move
12

– The Hourglass
14

– I Am
20

– Taynim
22

– Resuscitate
23

– Wisdom
28

– Seth
29

– Sunset
32

– Pay Attention
33

– Sending Secrets
34

– Without Praise
35

2 – Postcards from Venus
38

– A Message to True Love (Whoever You Are)
39

– Fool Addicted
41

– A Corner of Your Space
42

– If I Were You
44

– The Voice of a Woman
49

– One More fix
53

— Fool Addicted II
56

3 — Dear John (Your Name Here)
57

— About Doubt
58

— Maybe
62

— The Consequence
63

— Morning
66

— Cloud Keeper
68

— When?
70

— Unbroken Home
72

— The Awakening
73

— In an Instant
76

4 — Baggage Claim
78

— Back in the Day
79

- Homeless
  84

- Midnight Imposition
  87

- No One Saw a Thing
  89

- Boy Story (The Debriefing)
  91

- Forever Yours
  95

- The Devil in Black Face
  98

- Ms. Marva's One-side Spat with God
  100

- Too Many Roses
  103

- Old Man on the Corner
  105

- Gunpowder Scenes
  107

- Jezebel
  109

About the Author
115

Copyright © 2025 by Journey Johnson
All rights reserved. No part of this book may be reproduced in any manner whatsoever without written permission except in the case of brief quotations embodied in critical articles and reviews.
First Printing, 2025

...but to look back on the stony plain along the road which led on to that place, is not at all the same thing as walking on the road; the perspective, to say the very least, changes only with the journey;

only when the road has, all abruptly and treacherously, and with an absoluteness that permits no argument, turned or dropped or risen, is one able to see all that one could not have seen from any other place.

James Baldwin
Go Tell it on the Mountain Top

MIND TRAVELIN'

Necessary Journey

To go down deep inside myself
    In search of something more,
Something missing,
Something lost-
Somewhere

I stagger on the precipice of being,
Undaunted and afraid;
I fling myself headlong
Into my core.

Intently, I descend
To the bottom of it all

To face and then examine
All I dared not see,
To take a candle to the darkness
Of a long-abandoned me.

A Necessary Journey of the Soul...

Window Revelations

I inject into daydreams
   Metaphoric morphine,
Flooding the air of plight-mares
Like moonbeams
Pierce shadows of the darkest night.

I'm a hype
Feinding the fix of my poetry pipe.

Praying to a Goddess I have felt but not seen,
And rumors that I never will
Send a hot flash of cold chills.
I gotta pop another verse pill,
Snort a rhyme line and sit still.

Looking over windowsills
I see the tops of rolling hills
I'll never climb,
They play on my mind-

Tempting-
Like Christ to a Christian.
Calling collect
Demanding submission.
Keep wishin'.

I deny the charge and slam the phone,

JOURNEY JOHNSON

Sending inebriated echoes through the halls
Of my contemplative queen-dome.
Nobody's home.

I journey alone on my mission;
No time for hills,
I've mountainous visions.

Poetic incisions cut fine lines on the mind.
Dreamscapes to climb,
I set the clock on rewind,
Buying more time
To ponder decisions.

Shall I believe what I read?
Submit and concede
To a mutated breed?

Say to the order- *Yes, I believe*
In the manipulative lie babies
You have conceived.

Get down on my knees
And indeed
Beg a favor of the blue-eyed savior?

Oh, please, would he please?
Forgive my savage sins
And dry the torrential tears I cry?

Pull a number, take a ticket for a try

NECESSARY JOURNEY

At the pearly gates and testify,
While I do time in welfare lines?

Beg their god to fill my cup
Til it runneth over with white lies
And dumb drops?

I think not.
They got me fucked up.

I accept nothing from oppressors
Imposing beliefs like coke lines
And peer pressure.

Not religion nor reasons
For statues on dressers,
They wage war on the world
And call *us* aggressors.

And though I strive to live life
Color blind,
Racism scars leave
Braille on the mind.

I finger the lessons
Of history and time,
Searching for reasons
My kind's in decline.

Ah...here it is.
First chapter, line seven, verse nine;

JOURNEY JOHNSON

They took our ladders for their own
And left us cob webs to climb.

Got me dangling from threads
Between the living and the dead
Replaying in my head
The words the preacher man said
When I was a babe
With little bows on my head.

No warning of the poison
I was to be fed.
Like countless sheep before me
To the slaughter I was led
When he said

God said,
Before any of His children shall sit
On the sidewalk and beg bread,
Heaven and earth shall pass away.
Is what he said.

Should have said
To the girl I was, with bows on my head,
That hope was dead.
Should have put a bullet in my head.

Should have seen the breath I bled
As I step from the pew
To the aisle that led
Out of the door

NECESSARY JOURNEY

Of that Little Lie Shed
Into a flood of the living dead.

Murdered from birth
By the thoughts in their head.
Sidewalks awash with
The beggars of bread.

Through the sweltering stench of the smell
Befell the piercing screams of a rebel yell.
Reason provoked and rhetoric repelled,
Logic propelled through the wailing of anger. She said

If you believe what was read,
Then earth is demolished, and heaven has fled
And we are dwellers of hell, blood-fire red.
To the destitute souls out begging for bread.

For the dead amongst living,
For the starved amongst fed,
I spat out the poison
My old self was shed.

Slipped my grip from the cob webs
And burnt down the stairs,
No longer inclined to bind
What's mine to what's theirs.

They say, *Silky is sexy*,
Dread the locs in my hair.
They want silent consent,

JOURNEY JOHNSON

I send screams through the air.

Insight insurrections.
Turn their dreams to plight-mares
'Cause I'm staring into shadows
Of an empty page.

Taking pen to paper,
I fill it with rage.
Flying through thought
Like a bird too long caged.

I'm engaged on the
Stage of my mind.
Looking at foothills,
Seeking mountains to climb.

Riding moonbeams of inklings
To heights beyond high.
Injecting metaphoric morphine
Into poetry pipes.

Lacing my veins with lyrical rain,
Easing the pain of living mundane.
Seeing mountains in foothills
Over windowpanes,
Inhaling a breath
I can't claim.

I have to free my mind
So my soul can follow.

NECESSARY JOURNEY

Find the serum of delirium
And take my last swallow.

OD on poetry and write again
Tomorrow.

The End of Patience

She made him of her flesh,
    Nourishing him
In the bountiful fruit of her bosom
Until he stood erect.

And then he forgot her.
Disregarded and degraded her.
Stifling her breath until it hung
Heavy and gray and impure.

All he made came to desecrate
Her sacred pools of life,
And all other offspring of her flesh
Suffered and died
Because he forgot her.

And even when she wept for him,
He cared not to remember.
Her tears came in torrents,
Her rage hurled the winds of her breath
To destruction.
Yet she remained forgotten.

Then one morning
He looked through his penthouse window
With the ocean view,
But there was no ocean

NECESSARY JOURNEY

And there was no view.

Only the gaping serpentine tear
In the flesh of the womb
He was born of.

And she called for him
And he went to her,
And she consumed him.
And he would never forget her
Again.

They Move

They move in acquiescence
    Under southern skies,
Parting no waters,
Moving no mountains,
But they move.

Antiquated spirits long for lands before.
For times preceding chains,
Proceeding foreign shores,
Yet they move.

Leaving kings and farmers,
Departing queens and brides.
Arriving beasts of burden
On a blood-stained eastern tide,
And they move.

With grand resilience before iniquity.
Owning no country,
Building a country.
How they move!

With backs as strong as steel
And faith profound in the surreal,
They move.

To rise again as heaven's men

NECESSARY JOURNEY

To never let it be again,
They move.

With spirits yet unbroken
And tales to tell of the unspoken,
They move.

To spare their seeds from living in
The sweltering hell they had been in,
So they move

In acquiescence under southern skies,
Parting no waters,
Moving no mountains,
But they move.

Yes, they move.

The Hourglass

Tic Toc,
    It's 10:11 on the
Dot

And I've been listening to the

Tic
Chase the
Toc

Since the penny and the dime
Shagged the nine.

I reminisce, I reminisce
From time to time.
Explore a memory,
Then rewind.

All the while and all the way
With every breath I
Breathe away.
I'm listening to the

Tic
Chase the
Toc

NECESSARY JOURNEY

Watching
Crystals of my past
Slipping through the hourglass.
There they go again.

I wonder

How many grains of time
Are at the top?
How many precious breaths
Before they stop?

It's 10:13
Now
'56

I'm watching sparrows
Pick up sticks
To build themselves
A home. A throne.
A nest. A shelter.

It's Helter Skelter
For the homeless.

The null and voided,
The twice-exploited.
Every spirit
Needs a home.

To rest the weary bones

JOURNEY JOHNSON

That tread the constant tides alone.

I hear the moans
Of a thousand restless souls.
They roam,
Searching for the shore of restoration.

My heaven is a nation
Of past and future generations.
No Black, No White,
No pigmentation
Only salvation.

Welcome, welcome
To the kingdom of Zion.
Fear not. Fear
The Conquering Lion.

Moving through the realm of gold horizons
He is your shoulder to cry on,
Your faith to rely on.
Drive on, strive on
He's coming forth to carry you home.

So, drown not
In the tears you've cried,
And tread not
In the ceaseless tide.
Stand up, my love,
And cast aside your pride.

NECESSARY JOURNEY

You're in the palm of Father's hands.
You're only human,

A single crystal grain of sand
Slipping through the hourglass,
Watching futures turn to past
And listening to your

Tic
Chase your
Toc

Why?

The past has been spent,
It's true.
It was only lent
To you.

You borrowed it,
Put off until tomorrow'd it.
Don't stress yourself about where
It went.

It's gone.
Say so long
And carry on
Cause you'll never get it back.

Get on your knees, in fact,
Retract and implore.

JOURNEY JOHNSON

Beg the Father for more.

Crystal minutes,
Grains of time,
But there's a wait,
So get in line.

Forget regret,
There's no time,
There's no time.
It's a mess.

You'd best confess and digress.
Ponder how you failed the test
Trying to feed the emptiness
With earthly material.
But the hunger was ethereal,
And tricks are for cereal.

You dig?

Wantonness kills the flesh
And desecrates the soul.
You dug yourself a hole,
Lived your life like a mole;
Blind to your surroundings.

You had no spiritual grounding.
So when the trumpet blew,
You knew
Nothing.

NECESSARY JOURNEY

Nothing but the cars you drove
And the backs you rode.
Now erode.
Back to sand and crystal grains.

There's nothing under
Heaven's sky to gain.
The fact remains,

Here we are.
Every bruise
Every scar.

Watching crystals of our past
Slipping through the hourglass
And wondering...

How many grains of time
Are at the top?
How many blessed breaths
Before they stop?

Tic...
Toc.

I Am

I am the darkness,
　I am the light.
I am the moon
Against the night.

A mind ethereal,
A form earthbound.
The awkward silence
In the sound.

And in the breeze
Of morning's glory,
I write the verse
Of twice-told stories.

But the words,
The words are not enough.
And the voice,
The voice is not enough

To make you
Feel me.
Truly
Feel me.

I am the Journey
And the end.

NECESSARY JOURNEY

The nemesis,
The long-lost friend.

I am the warmth,
The hollow chill.
I am the ever
Present will.

To go on,
To know on.
To grow on,
To flow on.

I am.

Taynim

When I fall into the onyx seas that are your eyes,
    Your love becomes my everything
And I am enrapt.

When my eyes are blinded by the sun
That is your smile,
My heart leaps for the heavens
And I am irretrievable.

When my fingers swim the endless
Oceans of your curls,
Once more, I find myself
Blissfully adrift.

And then I hear the symphony that is your voice,
And it frolics through my mind;
I love you, Mama.

And in that moment, ever so briefly,
I let myself come back again
To say

I love you, too.

Resuscitate

Breathe in,
    Breathe out,
Exhale, my love;
Don't suffocate.

Resuscitate, Sistah, resuscitate.

Once upon a time, we climbed
Mountains high enough
To cause rain showers,
And we bathed in it.

Now Goddess finds
We sign our souls upon the line
In Babylonian chump towers,
And we are played in it.

The bed was made
And now we lay in it.
And lose our way in it.

So very many days
Have found us
Slayed in it.

In subtle little ways,
We've *all* been

JOURNEY JOHNSON

Paid in it.

Candlelight by moonlight,
Ignite the ghost arrayed in it.
Victoria's secrets
Been betrayed in it.

Tears on our pillow,
Pills and we're still low,
So now we pray
In it.

Answers spread like cancer
Through the demon's dirty dancer,
Hear the message play
And replay in it.

Breathe in,
Breathe out,
Exhale, my love;
Don't suffocate.

Resuscitate, Sistah, resuscitate.

Don't *stay* in it.

Once upon a time, we shined the light
On an unilluminated world.

Day glow Black Pearls unfurled
As we twirled universal swirls

NECESSARY JOURNEY

Through the short little curls
Of our chocolate Milky Ways.
A star is born every day in this way.

Ethereal erections
Metaphysical injections
Creation is perfection
For it is born of the womb, man.

Now, Goddess finds our kind consumed
By those who presume.
She who worships natural law
Should be riding a broom.

While superhero zeros
Run boardrooms like cartoons.
Ka blam and Ka boom!
God damn! Bad Man!
Give a Sistah room

To breathe in,
Breathe out,
Exhale, my love;
Don't suffocate.

Resuscitate, Sistah, resuscitate.

Once upon a time
We owned our minds,
But the demons, they hated it.

JOURNEY JOHNSON

Careened our Self-esteem
And deflated it
Because they hated it.

Could not beseech our speech
To preach what they teach,
So they berated it.
Nearly mutated it
Because they hated it.

Couldn't win the skin we are in
So they raped and segregated it
Because they hated it.

Could not use like mules
The culturally fused.
So they ascended
Like vultures in crews
And devastated,
Because they hated it.

Take no pity on fools
Who take our world for their jewel,
For we created it.

History books are nooks for crooks
Who perpetrated it.
PG-13 is how they rated it.

Parental Guidance Strongly Suggested
To wrongly ingest and

NECESSARY JOURNEY

Perpetuate the shit.

But I have seen
That scene before,
Must say
I hated it.

I waste no time on flat lines,
But I am stating it.
Take your Self off life support,
Support your life,
Start elevating 1t.

Breathe in,
Breathe out,
Exhale, my love.
Don't suffocate.

Resuscitate, Sistah, resuscitate.

Wisdom

Does not
   Send out echoes
From a mountain top.

It does not
Dazzle us with feathers
Bold and grand

Or beat its chest in victory
Over brothers slain
In ignorance.

It whispers gently
Through the heart
And leaves tear drops
On the soul.

Seth

You and I were one once,
    In a million other lifetimes,
Exiting the Garden
Goddess blessed me your appointment.

You would call me later, Isis
And answer to the name of Pharaoh.

I hear, still, your footsteps
Tracing the halls of the pyramids,
Cultivating civilization's oyster.
But you, son, are its pearl.

I hailed you,
Kamehameha.

Out of legions you made one,
You ruled our Polynesia
As life is ruled by sun.
King of compassion,
Servant of none.

Ka`ahumanu kissed you gently
And your people remain reverent
Of the Lonely King.

I held you, Seth,

JOURNEY JOHNSON

At the docks of Virginia

And venom seethes my heart,
Still trapped in the bowels of Tecora
Vainly. Desperately
Protecting you
From what is yet
Our greatest tragedy.

Teardrops and buck shots
Flood my mental hot spots.
I remember the lynching of Denmark Vesey
After the insurrection.

You ran like the wind,
Pulling brethren behind you,
Shouting, *Fuck your institution!*
Before slipping into the shadows
To freedom.

Even then, you were the revolution.

I knew you, too,
At Birmingham

Dogs and water hoses a muck.
You spat in the face of injustice
When you spat in the face of that cop.
For your rise was the prize.

From Civilizations pearl

NECESSARY JOURNEY

Beyond the Civil Rights world
Your shine remains constant.
You are the northern light.

Seth,
You and I were one once,
In a million other lifetimes.
In flesh we meet again.

How my soul soars in anticipation.
Which dominions will you claim?
An infinite king in ascension,
The world is yours to reign.

As in every precious lifetime,
I am here with you.
Go forward, son, to destiny,
But care not to forget

Sow along your journey on
The seeds of righteousness,
They'll be your next life's blessing,
As sure as Goddess sees.

You and I are one, son,
For all eternity.
I love you,
Mama.

Sunset

Outside my window
    The sun seethes blood red
In the warm summer's breath
Of the dusk,
And cacti stand in praise
Among defiant desert flesh.

Outside my window
Rust orange skies compete
With dust-powder blues and high yellow golds
For the unappeasing eye
Of the unseeing.

For if only *one*,
Just one
Solitary soul
Or single spirit dwelling
Should ever care to see,

They would surely witness
The omnipotent bellow
And undying love
Of creation.

Pay Attention

Life loves the liver,
   And disregard the myth.
Just because you're breathing
Don't mean you're living it.

Love loves the lover,
But this ain't always true.
'Cause just because you're loving Love
Don't mean Love's loving you.

Though dreams love the dreamer,
It's important that I say
The dreams you dream within the night
You must actualize in the day.

Now friends love the friendship,
But this is what I've found
The truest test of friendship
Comes when you've fallen down.

Of all these things I've spoken,
The crucial lies herein,
What you cast out on the ocean
The tides will sure bring in.

Sending Secrets

When you see her humbled on the street,
    A fallen angel at your feet,
Dirtied skin and matted hair,
Dispirited and barely there.

Sharing secrets with herself,
Don't hasten thoughts to something else.

Listen

Don't pretend to check your watch,
Don't speed your pace another notch.

Just listen.

Assess the cryptic monologue
Floating through her mystic fog
For the winds that broke her wings
May send your way those very things.

Wise ones know that heaven rings
In the secrets angels sing.

Listen.

Without Praise

Without praise or accolade,
    I defend my mind-glades
Against midnight-mare raids
And attacks at nerve break.

Retract for my sake and
Without reward or recognition,
Hot wire admissions
From Black Hawks downed
With chalk in my pockets.
To outline the flat-lined who
Have declined my rhythm rockets.

Man-grenades in hand,
I expand thoughts in cockpits
And cause those with the balls to explode.

Rewind view-find,
Release and unload.
Downloads like classes
Unto the uncivil innocence
Of the masses.
The pass
To surpass this-

Take off my glasses
And

JOURNEY JOHNSON

Without haste or a chaser,
Drink Gillespie gulps of truth serum,
Then lie in the trenches of deceit.

Repeat. Repeat
Do not retreat!

The world at my feet like a fleet,
I see battles shipwreck the weak,
And the earth shall devour the meek.

I am a creek without a paddle,
Yet I leak streams of dreams
Into ways and means
When I speak

Without prompt or permission.
My mission?
Submissions of mental emissions
Into the mentally imprisoned
With such precision
I cause visions.

Further blur the slurred exterior
Of rhythm and reading
Until the venue is bleeding
And the hungry are eating
The followed preceding
From the palm of my hands.

NECESSARY JOURNEY

With or without a mic or a stand,
I supply on demand the core of contraband
As I slam into every woman and man
Within reach

The Freedom of Speech.

POSTCARDS FROM VENUS

A Message to True Love (Whoever You Are)

I'll wait for you
    Where stars fall into seas of iridescent light
And angels glide on crystal wings
Eternally in flight,
And love is not taboo.

Where liquefied desires
Flow in currents irretrievable
And passion pirouettes
Where deceit is inconceivable
Is where I'll wait for you.

For many are temptations
Masquerading destiny,
And many, too, are broken hearts,
Wilting in reality,
For they were never you.

When opal moons glow over valleys
Of entities untold,
And waterfalls fall upward,
Through heavens made of gold,
You'll come for me,

And I will have known you

For eternity.
Until then, my love,
I'll wait for you.

Fool Addicted

If I had known that forever
   Meant til the morning,
And hell would descend on my world
Without warning,
I would have kissed you still.

If I had a clue that my heart
Would break without fight,
And my body succumbed
To a thief in the night
Beneath my windowsill.

I would have loved you
The same-
Played fool
To your game.

I am an addict
Of the thrill.

A Corner of Your Space

If I only had a corner of your space
   I'd replace the empty spaces
With traces of moonbeam love scenes
In the evergreen shadows of your sun, hon.

If I could only be the one
Who spun the rhythm to your groove,
I'd remove and make smooth
Every stumble in your step,
Every Stutter in your stride
As we glide through your corridor of thought.

Picking locks of doors, forgot,
Finger painting Renoir memoirs
On your contemplative hot spots.
Slipping the drip drops of forget-me-nots
Along the dotted line of your spine.

Surreal...sublime...serpentine-
I entwine your mind in a cerebral slow grind.
Too divine to define.
So thin is the line,

The ripple...the seam
Between Spirit and Dream.
It seems to convene, then erase in a haste
Our phantom embrace.

NECESSARY JOURNEY

I trance in this space
Enhance in this space
Romance in this space,
A smile on my face,
Amazed in your grace

Before I erase,
Leaving no trace
That I was ever in
A corner of your
Space.

If I Were You

She asked me
   So told her.

And this is what was said,
As I looked into her eyes
And ran my fingers
Through her hair.

She said,
What would you do,
If you were me, making love
To you?

I thought she'd never ask.
I said,

If I were you, making love to me
Pleading hands on silken flesh
Would cause a train's derailment,
And love would know no death.

For your breath
And my breath,
Like our breath,
Would flow

Gently

NECESSARY JOURNEY

In circles
Around us.

If I were you, making love to me
A hastened pulse would signal
The rebirth of Dionysus,
And ecstasy would gain meaning
Once more.

For your breath
And my breath,
Swirling in circles
Around us

Would quicken at the thought of
All the things you've seen
And all the places you've been-
Between my
Sheets.

And the breeze of our breath,
Swirling through time,
Would remind us of thirst
Never quenched.

Drenched, now we'd drink
From the fountains of love
And the rivers of life
Until our lips dripped with sins
Never spoken

JOURNEY JOHNSON

And our minds would drown in
This ocean of greed,
Like two hungry children unfed.

And then she moved her lips to speak,
But I said,
Hush, darlin',

If I were you, making love to me,
My tongue would taste of wine.
Real wine...

Pinot Noir or Merlot,
Cabernet Sauvignon.
Not this tootie fruity bullshit.

And it would roll like thunder
At the parting of my thighs,
Licking clean the cream from my lips
And the sweat from my neck.
Let's reflect

If I were you, making love to me
The moon would eclipse the sun
When buttons came undone
Of course, I'd run.

But you'd catch me
And ask me
Whose it was,
And I'd tell you

NECESSARY JOURNEY

Whose it is,

And the sounds of submission
Would penetrate the swirling of breath
All around us.

And the dimming blue light
Above our bed
Would grow even dimmer still
Against the fleeting flashes of pain
In the pleasure of love.

If I were you, making love to me
There'd be no "*ifs*" to speak of.

We'd love like tomorrow
Was ours to behold
And I'd be held in your arms
For a lifetime.

Rewind

To the beginning of the thought.
To the beginning of the thought,
To the beginning.

Girl...

I thought it was you
Making love to me,
With pleading hands

And fleeting breath,
Dionysus brought back from death.

I thought it was you making love to me
When my lips were dripping
With the sins of intoxication,
And redemption came only
From loving you.

Beneath the dimming blue light,
Surrounded by the sound
And fleeting flashes of pain
In the pleasure of love.

It was you making love
It was you making love
It was you.

Making love

To
Me.

The Voice of a Woman

Haunts my thought patterns
   Like rings around Saturn,
Leaving shadows on the lips
Of poor Venus.

For she has never seen this.
This
Pause,
And then
Stop
Of her heart.

No longer a choice is
The echoes of voices
That ricochets against
The stars of her eyes
Causing me to cry
Whole soul tears,
Longing to hear
That voice.

The voice of a woman
Seers like the sun,
This one unsuspecting-
Genuflecting-
In her light years.

JOURNEY JOHNSON

Too drawn to the flame for U-turns
I burn incense sticks and
Candle wicks at both ends,
Trying to see my way out,
Still smelling like a rose.

No one knows the shows
That go on in surround sound
When she is around,

For I glow head to toe,
And compose like a pro
The facade of composure.

My northern exposure
Is witnessed by one
And she is the one

Who can shun and dismiss
At the drop of a hat
My heart's pitter-pat.
Imagine that.

And I lay track after track
Of burnt bridges behind me
And never look back.

Not that
It's a choice.
I am drawn to that voice.

NECESSARY JOURNEY

It soothes me,
Even when she bruises me
With a ...click.

Biting my lip
I still trip on my tongue
As I stare at the hung
Phone.

No right mind condones self-denial,
So at my reasoning trial, I plead guilty
To longing in the first degree
For the voice of this woman.

And sentence myself in cursed verses
To solitary confinement.
My daily assignment:
Self-refinement and improvement.

Don't think it. Prove it
I dare myself,
Compare myself
To the spiritual wealth I find rare.
Will I ever get there?

Even as I stare at the glare
Of pages before me,
My childlike rages implore me.

And I can see the flashes of
Backslashes and underscored dashes

Of her smashing existence.
Right here's my admission;

I read between the lines,
As she leaves caps locked signs
For my caution.

Somewhere in there,
Between snatching me from piercing stares
And bedroom declares of confessions,
I know that it's there.

And between laughter and pouts
And deep breaths of air
Drawn through tears,
A purpose endears
And paths become clear.

I may hear it.
The voice of a woman.

One More fix

Take a sip of the drip from my lips
One more kiss

Slip my grip from your hips as I dip
Tell me this...

How many twists of my fingers and wrists
Until there's bliss?

You resist
Yet there's mist where we mingle and mix.

One more night

In your eyes, I see stars as I fall from your sky.
Wish I might

Be wrapped tight and delight in your thighs.
Take a bite

Ever slight is the fight
Tell me why?

Dim the light
And take flight through the black and white truth

JOURNEY JOHNSON

As we lie
Still as night

Long as day, let me play in the rays of your sun.
Let me run

Index
Middle
Tongue

Through the fields of your dreams til you cum
Don't you *move*

Just begun.

One by one comes undone
Every thread on the web you have spun.

Round I go
On the merry-go-round of your soul.

Find the gold at the end of your rainbow.
Take it

Slow

So you know every jewel you are worth
You are Earth.

You are sun
You are moon

NECESSARY JOURNEY

You are first

To quench thirst as you burst
I consume every drop unrehearsed

Hit reverse
And beg this

One more fix

Take a sip from the drip of my lips.

One more kiss...

Fool Addicted II

If I had thought for one minute
   That I'd be caught in it
This tangled web we weave-

I would have come to you, willing,
Prepared for the thrilling
Erotic minds conceive.

The rush of loving, so sweetly
Yet ever discreetly,
The keeper of a dream.

The torrid desire
Only love could inspire
When whispers turn to screams.

If I had sensed you addictive
And known love vindictive,
I'd still not stand a chance

Against wanting so deeply,
And falling completely,
A fool to this romance.

CHAPTER 3

DEAR JOHN (YOUR NAME HERE)

About Doubt

Doubt dripped from her lips
    And unto the sunny afternoons
She'd prayed for.

The impurity of insecurity
Displayed more
Like Pay-Per-View on her stage.

Scripts lip through the scrolls of her mind,
And on cued time
Roll like a worn and weary monologue
Off her tongue

Which, just last night
Hung onto the stem of my fruit
Until the juice was enough to
Quench her thirst for my truth serum.

Now, she has to laugh,
Because it's all so sad how she sees
Right through me.

Through all my tired little games
And all my clever little ways
Of spending my God-forsaken days
Deceiving her.

NECESSARY JOURNEY

And I am thoroughly believing her
When she says
I'm like everyone else who has come
And gone.

I bet she sawed through them
Like she seers through me,

Until she sees nothing at all
But the ghost who haunt
The mirrored walls

She has installed for her defense
And adorned with the pretense
Of a good time girl.

So we swirl
To the rhythm of the groans in her head
That can only be silenced
By the moans in her bed
My hands on her head
And thighs on her cheeks.

This Is A Public Service Announcement:
The followed preceding is not for the weak
Or the faint of heart.

It speaks
To the down and dirty bleakness
Of the meekest existence.

JOURNEY JOHNSON

Self-destruction is the art
Of killing dreams before they start.

Had I been smart,
I would have seen the pieces of her
Explosive disposition
When she positioned psychic intuition
Between
Me, my Self
And self-esteem.

I mean.

The strokes of her tainted brush
Colored me bad,
And had I any sense but the jewel
Of my heart,
I would have ended the nightmare
Before the dream started
To unravel.

Never too late!
I slam the gavel
Of her cross-examination of me,
Mentally.

For I've learned the
Long, slow lesson of
Feeling free to talk about anything.

Burned in

NECESSARY JOURNEY

Long slow sessions
Beneath the swing of her
20/20 watt bulb.

Resolves dissolves
Like antacid on my tongue
And I swallow contempt
Like a chaser.

Was my loving a waste?
For her anger and haste
Has me erased.
As she cuts and she pastes
Every past name and face
In my place,

And blurs with her words
The last of my worth,
Until she sees nothing
In these panties and shirt
But hurt.

Maybe

If I try hard enough,
   Perhaps I could believe
That I never truly loved you-
That I never really grieved

For the heaven that we lost
At the too expensive cost

Of loving so strong
And needing so much,
The kindling of our spirits,
The longing in our touch.

Maybe if I dry these tears,
Try not to think of all those years

I spent loving you
With all my heart,
Maybe then
I could start

To forget you.

The Consequence

So you're standing here before me
    And I can't believe my ears,
And I can't fight for the life of me
The stinging of my tears;

You're leaving me today.

I can see your lips are moving,
And I long to steal a kiss,
And I haven't heard a single word,
For all I know, is this

You're leaving me today.

And I want so much to stop you,
But I can't 'cause I'm afraid,
Lest I become unraveled
And my foolishness displayed/\.

You're leaving anyway.

Now I see you coming to me,
And there's pity in your eyes,
And I hear myself say calmly
No tone of my demise.

In the words I say.

JOURNEY JOHNSON

It's not as if I never knew
Of your child...and your wife.
And I swallow them like venom-
Your child and your wife.

You're going home today.

And your heart was never mine.
And your love was never mine.
And the love we made within the night
Was not the loving kind,

And you never came to stay.

Now, I lock the door behind you
As I try to understand
How I let my feelings marry
An already married man

Who only came to play.

And I walk through every room
And I unplug every phone,
Trying to salvage what is left
Of my dissipating home.

And then I stop to say,

To the woman in the mirror,
Who weeps in front of me,

NECESSARY JOURNEY

Who I never thought I would become
Until temptation tempted me,

I'm leaving *you* today.

Morning

Midnight threatens me
   It's gaping hollow
And I'm afraid to go.

Again,
I'll be alone.

Narcissistic suitors
Linger aloof
Outside my door.

Mirrors in hand,
They come
And go.

I'd rather be alone.
If I could just
Climb inside this
Glass of Pinot Noir

Drown myself inside its
Temporary anesthesia,
I could make it
I'm sure-

To the sweet embrace
 Of

Morning.

Cloud Keeper

When the clouds hung above me
    In desolate gloom,
You said to me,
It's going to be all right.

But from the corner
Of my mind's eye
I saw it,
Silent content in your smile.

As I lay gasping,
Grasping for life's sweet air,
You breathed inside of me
Your gentle breeze.

But I could have sworn

I felt the faintest tips of your fingers
Slightly...tightly...constricting
Around the flesh of my throat.

And now those clouds have parted,
For my sun has finally come,
But you say to me

That sun is not for you, and
That light is not your light.

NECESSARY JOURNEY

And I hear the prayers you send,
Bring back the clouds again.

When?

I don't know exactly
   When it happened
Or when it all began,

When I stopped being
Your future,

And instead became
Your fool.

The callused twist of fate
Sent our love

On a
Downward
Spiral.

And while you managed
To remain aloft,

I plummeted endlessly
After desperation and
Desperate acts

Removed me from
Your pedestal
And replaced me

NECESSARY JOURNEY

In your past.

I see
Indeed,
It happened.

All I ask is...

When?

Unbroken Home

Forget the way I held
   You together

When the world around you
Fell apart.

Dismiss the thoughts
Of loving me.

Put me out
Of your heart.

Then pretend you couldn't care less
When she asks you if you do.

I'll be waiting here for you.
Come home when you're through.

The Awakening

Whirling a million miles a minute,
    I see my sanity
Burning blue-black cyclonic streaks
Around me.

My optic corridors are whitewater rapids,
Refusing to rush forward.
Refusing to undam the god-damned tears
I have collected over the years.

Big girls don't cry... Shit
Only every time you walk away.

I pray

That you might turn around
And see me turning flips for you.

Look at me!, I shout in silence
I am the fruit you picked out of greed.
You didn't need me.
Yet you ate me to the core.

And greed is never satisfied,
So you're off to pick some more.
The truest definition of a whore
I have ever seen.

JOURNEY JOHNSON

Getting paid in orgasms of tears,
Tears that quench your thirst somehow,
Tears that feed your appetite.

I wish I may, I wish I might
Shed a thousand tears tonight.

I close my eyes,
Trying to bring the rain.
Yet and still, despite the pain,
I cannot cry.

Why?

My mind is too full to cry.
My heart is too full to cry.
The well is too deep to ever run dry,
But the tears will not come.

How come?

Because a lifetime
And a thousand tears ago
I was your life.
Your future wife.

Now I struggle to free
My mind from the knife
Bringing strife to my thoughts,

NECESSARY JOURNEY

And I see my sanity
Burning blue-black cyclonic streaks
Around me.

This is the awakening.

In an Instant

In an instant, like a blink, set
   In suspension.
From beyond this dimension to the third, I
Inhale his exhale, and give birth to death.

And through the cum shot
And the blood clot
I see no regret—
Not just yet.

Destiny does not subject herself
To intellect or introspect.
She simply injects the meta into physics
Until she gets what she sets.

Destiny cannot be regretted by a mere mortal
Whose portal into immortality lies in Destiny's hands.
Who are we to make demands?

We're only human and
Suicidal tendencies tend to be
Destiny's way of regretting us.

A mother who wishes the child dead, but
Instead must hold herself to her self-imposed clause.
Grit her teeth. Set her jaws

NECESSARY JOURNEY

And impose upon reality universal laws.
I saw in his eyes the prize of the knowing.
I mean, they were glowing.

But his heart beat his ear
To a different drummer.
Destiny reached for his soul
But resistance tore spirits asunder.

His life port split way to welcome the cosmic
But reality proved comic.
He could not hear the message
Because he was not bionic,
And the sound was supersonic.

Like an instant, in a blink, set
In suspension
From beyond this dimension
To the third, I
Inhale his exhale
And give birth to death.

And through the cum shot
And the blood clot
I see no regret--
Not just yet.

BAGGAGE CLAIM

Back in the Day

Back in the day when I was young
    I'm not a kid anymore,
But sometimes
I sit and wish I were
A kid again.

Remember when
Dogs chased cats like pussy was power.
Wasn't nothin' like tin roofs and thunder showers.

Makin' love for hours
To the one you loved,
Sunday mornin' spoon hugs
On an island in the sea.

See? Those were the dazes
When brown-eyed girls in purple hazes
Captured the gazes
Of eyes set afire, but never burned in the blazes
Like these modern-day crazes,
Which I pray are just phases,

I mean,

It amazes the senses.
Nonsense is intense at the expense
Of the pussy.

JOURNEY JOHNSON

Pussy controlled power is now,
Power controlled pussy, somehow.
Like power locks and power windows
Just flash the master's card
And in like Flynn you go-

Legs rise on cue like garage doors.
And if you're drivin' a Lexus or Benz,
Then... hell, tell a friend!
Ain't no need to pretend.
We're all adults here.

And it ain't your fault, dear.
Your mama raised you wrong
Is what it is.

Fact is, she shoulda splain'd you bettah
Because the mind, not the money,
Should get the pussy wettah
Yet ah...dear Joe in a Jetta
Can't get a John lettah.

And the better half of chicken heads
Are gathered together in the light of the club.
Paid for outright right there at the pub.

Lookin' good and good at lookin'
Man hollers at his buddy,

Gimme daps, Pap

NECESSARY JOURNEY

Ain't no hap's, Jack,
I'll be right back
I'm just gon'
Choke the chicken.

Time keeps on tic'n, tic'n.
Into the first and fifteenth,
Clockwork like the mail run
Sun, sleet, or shower.

Just say hell to wedding bells,
Cancel the flowers.

Cause if the whip is tight enough,
Then Mister's right enough
And can get pussy...
By the hour.

And if to whom you give your pussy
Is to whom you give your power

On behalf of Motel 6's
I'd like to thank the little bitches
Who have made them what they are today.

Next to Ho-Jo's, the biggest receptacle
Of disrespectable pussy in America.

They salute you,
While niggahs pollute you.
Say, *You were a hoot, boo,*

JOURNEY JOHNSON

Then give you the boot, too.

Too bad you never had the proper upbringing,
And if you had

Too bad you only heard the
Cha-chingin' of the pimps blingin'
So bright you never saw your mama's eyes stingin',
Watchin' your babies watch you do your thing-thing,

And the thing about it is tragic.
The magician's sellin' her magic.
The statement I make is emphatic
That's it, that's all.
I'm through with this planet.

Star date: 2002, 2/15 at 1:13
Journey's log:
Beam me up, Scotty,
Pussy's gone to the dogs.

And the gods must be fallen
Or fled,
Because the almighty pussy
Has given to head.

And all hope is dead
Because she, who led nations,
Now follows.
And she, who was hand-fed
Now swallows.

NECESSARY JOURNEY

And if things keep going on this way,
There'll be no pussy tomorrow.
Just a teen aged mutant breed of bitches,
Hateful and hollow.

My heart, full of sorrow's ablaze
As I fixate my gaze in the haze,
Searchin' the maze.

Reachin'
Back for the days when I was young.
I'm not a kid anymore

But sometimes
I sit and wish I were
A kid again.

Homeless

Smoke gray clouds envelope
   Shimmering skyscrapers,
Still managing to radiate in all this
Dreariness.

In weariness,
Thousand-dollar suits
And the latest designer skirts
Scuttle through
Ice wet droplets,
Falling with relentless
Sarcasm onto the city streets.

Where

Coffee shops,
Coffee shops,
Coffee shops.

Shelter the masses,
Consumed with their classes.
In cavalier crassness.
They Marinate.

In aromas of double-shot espressos
And cinnamon cappuccinos,
Tall and skinny

NECESSARY JOURNEY

Assaulting the many
Notes of the homeless.

Too void of money to buy a cup,
Too void of self to once look up,
They dissipate

To a mere backdrop
Of this blasé scene.

I've seen that every corner holds one.
Every alleyway.

Some poor soul awaits for you
To coolly turn away
His plea for change.

Change, you claim, with
Even cooler annoyance
Not to have.

Must have
Spent it all on that Nordstrom bag.
Or is it Eddie Bauer?

My, how you cower
At the thought of lending him a hand.
He's a disgrace to man.

And yet

JOURNEY JOHNSON

He was once someone's brother,
Man.
Someone's lover,
Man.
Someone's father,
Man.

He's once seen brighter days,
Now his spirit pays day to day.
Who of us can say
There's no way
He could have ever been us?

Once upon a time,
Doing fine, sipping wine
Until it all came down

Hardship and tribulation.
As relentless as the icy rain,
One after the other,
Onto the next

Until enough
Was too much.

And he laid down his burden
Giving in to the failure
That threatens
Us all.

Midnight Imposition

Jagged hands on wilting flesh
    Force themselves up weary thighs.
Unwanted.
Unsolicited.

Harshness orphans bended knees
Of each other's
Company.

And God
Has turned an eye
To another

Midnight imposition.

Delusion trembles greedy lips
To pull at tender breasts
In urgency.

One hand holds the wrists,
Too delicate
For twisting.

The other covers lips,
Never meant for
Kissing.

And stifled cries
Denote
Another

Midnight imposition.

No One Saw a Thing

Come when I call you, bitch!
　　And so it all began-
The bruising of an eye
By the raising of a hand.

But
No one saw a thing.
You see.
No one saw a thing.

No one saw the busted lip,
And no one saw the marks.
It happened falling down the stairs,
Her mechanical remark.

Since to appease a lie is easier
Than to seek the truth,
No one gave a mention
'Bout the newly missing tooth.

No one said a thing,
You hear?
No one said a thing.

No one queried when
She could not come to work.
And no one came to help, the night

JOURNEY JOHNSON

He finally went berserk.

No one called the cops, you know,
Not a finger touched the phone,
And no one slept at all,
The dawn Ms. Eva died alone.

And at the funeral
Later on that week,
No heads were lower bowed
Than those who dared not speak.

For their minds were all weighed heavy
With denial and with guilt.
And they all begged for forgiveness
From the soul they all helped kill.

Tragic.

They all knew of the blood
On each and every hand,
But no one said a thing,
And you must understand-

No one said a thing,
My love,
Cause no one
Gave a damn.

Boy Story (The Debriefing)

He can't take rejection
   Like he can't take the truth,
So his heedless erections
Leave seeds with no roots,
Like strange fruit.
That hang faceless from the laces
Of his discarded boots.

Worn thin from running
Through women
Whose only connection to him
Were reflections of him.

The mirrors made his mind swim
In the delirium of his reality.
He is emphatically a fallacy.
Existing callously in phallic seas.

Merely a casualty
Of delusions' drive-by.
Who survives by
His fly-by-nights
In life's support.

He can't revive by himself
And it kills him.
Wills him to set sail every dawn

For new ports to distort.

Leaving a maze of watery graves
In the misguided haze
Of his intruder nights
And Bermuda days.

Loveless triangles,
Entangled and mangled
In his murky depths
And shallow ways.

Can't love the one he's with,
So the ones who love him pay.
Copper top tear drops for a shot
At a guest appearance slot
In his disappearing
Act.

Fact is
There is always a sequel
In the making,
Always an equal
For the taking.

Always a new thrill
In the art of baby making,

Always a strong will to kill,
An arched back for the breaking.
And always a steeple on a hill

NECESSARY JOURNEY

To stop his God from forsaking
This sorry ass.

Ask him no questions,
He'll still tell a lie,
Then lie on his deathbed, wondering why,
Seeking truths in the sky.

Flashbacks forward
His last breath to this scene,
The brink of infinity
Revealed his Holy Trinity:
Money, Power, and Greed.

The keeper of his soul
Possessed the bluest eyes he'd ever seen,
And spoke unto the dying boy
Whispers soft and serene.

This is all you ever were
And all you've ever been.
You are the ends to our means,
The pawn in our scheme.

Willie lynched your daddy
But you made bitches of your queens.
Half the seeds you've planted
Daylight has never seen.

And the rest will only know you
Through the bling of movie screens.

JOURNEY JOHNSON

Hear you only through
A rapper's screams.

Retrace your every step
In sequential cliché scenes,
Chase coochie and cream like fiends
In your player pipe dreams.

Now you want to ask, why you?
What the fuck do you mean?
Bitch hoes like yourself is just what we need.
You're just the type of nigger
That'll wipe the Black race out clean.

You put your hand upon the Bible
And swore God was green.
Ben Franklin bought your spirit
And your soul left the scene.

Here's a shout out from your man, The Klan-
And daps from White Supremacy,
Thanks for leaving your seeds.
If they're anything like you, we'll soon be
Black Free.

Oh, here's a little postscript
That's an S after P.
Let this be our little secret.
Keep it
Between you and me.

Forever Yours

I impose uninvited
   A thief in your satin sheets;
I am the unexpected serum in your needle.
I am the hand that suffocates the innocence
Of your newborn baby boy.

Tender, precious baby boy.
Shame!

I dragged your cousin Anthony-
You know, the one y'all liked to call *queer*-
Kicking and screaming...and
Oozing and wheezing...and...
Shall I go on?

He did.

And bleeding and pleading
Until his final scab
Peeled way to death.

He was a handsome fellow, too,
And such a dreamer.
I'll bet you never thought he had it in him
To keep a secret like me.

Oh, I was in him all right,

But he never told a soul.
Not even his married preacher boyfriend,
Reverend Dr. James McNair.

Who shared (*as was his nature*),
Me with his wife, who
(In that same spirit of giving)
Passed me to that choirboy
Who mows their big old lawn.

Delicious!

Now choirboy had a sexy girlfriend
By the name of Gina Brown.
Y'all know the one
Perky lead pom-pomist
On the high school pom-pom squad

Who everybody's mama knows is as
Easy as apple pie.
Why, I imagine you can take it from there,
Cause I don't play hard to get.

The fact is, I'm quite easily acquired myself.
You don't even have to try,
And no one, honey,
Is immune to my highly
Infectious nature.

If you catch my drift.

NECESSARY JOURNEY

What gets me is your naive deficiency
In the matter of self-preservation.
Or should I say.... *What gets you!*
Indestructible, you are not.

You have what I like to call
An apathy syndrome,
But suit yourself.

I'll just come 'til I'm done
In epidemic proportions,
Until I am everywhere
You want to be.

Hear me?
Feel me?
Fear me.

The Devil in Black Face

I see him, Mama,
   Everywhere.
Listen.

Listen and you can hear his pleasure,
Because he's seen our future children,
And it's fading fast.

He's the Devil in Black Face, brother,
And he looks like you and me.
Take a look around you,
Tell me what you see.

He's out there on the corner,
Killing us slowly,
One by one by one,
Twenty sack at a time.

He's been doing it for years
And we haven't caught on yet.
Shit, maybe *niggahs* really are stupid
But I ain't a niggah. Hear me?

And neither are you.
Don't let him tell you different
Neither....are....you!

NECESSARY JOURNEY

The propaganda's spreading fast, though.
Check the radio. The dance hall's latest hit
Bitches poppin' pussies
And *hood rats* suckin' dicks.

Ain't nothin' but the Devil, sister,
The Devil in Black Face.
Don't dance for him no more.

Tell him, daddy, tell him.
Tell him that your daughters are not whores,
That your grandmas didn't scrub
Those kitchen floors

So he could thieve your sons
Of dreams and hope,
Watchin' cousins in the crack house
Sellin' dope.

Tell him, dammit, tell him.
Get him out.
Goddess,
Help us get him out.

Let us pray

Ancestors, please forgive us,
For we did not know
That the Devil merged the bluest eyes
With coffee skin and cornrows.

Ms. Marva's One-side Spat with God

Fatha', help me cuz I'm lost,
    Somewhere 'tween
Where it is I come from,
An' where it is I'm goin'.

Seems like I fell asleep one day
An' nevah woke back up.
But I mus' be woke,
Mus' be somethin'

Cuz I'm seein' errthang.
But I mus' be dreamin'
Bein' woke.
Cuz ain't nobody seein' me!

An' nobody's hearin' me,
An' nobody knows ma name!

Where it is dey goin?
Where dey comin' from?

Find me, Fatha', cuz I'm lost.

She drops her head and starts to cry.

NECESSARY JOURNEY

Somewhere `tween all I done
An' all I'm gon do,
An' I'm 'bout to lose ma mind.

A tear hangs on a sigh, exhaled through weary breath

An' I'm dirty.
Oooo-wooh! I'm dirty!
Or maybe deez folks is jus' too clean
I see 'um!

Spits at a distinguished passer-by

Lookin' down on me
Like I'm some kind of freak!
Some kind of...
Of..

There's a sudden darkness in her eyes,
A chilling bitter in her gaze,
And she's gone again
To oblivion.

Forget I even called you,
Bastard!

Mus' not be no kin to you.
Mus' be I ain't ya chile.
Else you'd of come an' got me by now
But that's all right.

JOURNEY JOHNSON

Who needs you?
Hell ain't all that bad.
I'm jus gon' go on back
To somewhere...

It's 'round here somewhere...
I'm sure.

Too Many Roses

You know, I see too many roses
    In combat boots,
In a weed-infested garden,
Being strangled at the roots.

Far too many roses
Being cut from our supply.
So venomous the thorns,
They go uncared for and denied.

While politicians lie
And parents question *why*
So few are they who try
One by one, they die.

Dance, little sister,
It ain't your fault.
You were ambushed into battle,
Unprepared for the assault.

You stood your round in fright,
In the chaos of the night;
You did not know the fight
Was one of mind, not might.
But now you know, and it's
All right.

JOURNEY JOHNSON

You are divine design;
Respect your flesh,
Expand your mind,
Explore your soul, and you may find
How well you blossom over time.

You really don't belong here, sis.
In the garden, you are queen.
Get your act together
So you can split this crazy scene.

Because I see too many roses
In combat boots,
In a weed-infested garden,
Being strangled at the roots.

Old Man on the Corner

I used to sit and watch him,
   And though I never knew his name,
I felt as if I knew him,
Knew him just the same.

Tall, and strong, and tender
Like a father would be,
I imagine..

Because I never knew my father,
And he never knew of me.

This stranger on the corner
Could be one and the same.
But I'll never come to ask him,
And I'll never know his name.

I used to wonder to myself
Who had he left behind?
This old man on the corner,
Begging change and passing time.

Did his world turn away
When he fell down?
Did his loved ones stray
When he lost ground?

JOURNEY JOHNSON

I wonder...

Where he lies
His head to sleep?
Does heaven know
Of this lost sheep?

I wonder...

When he dies
Who will care?
Will he pass
Like dust in air?

I wonder...

Gunpowder Scenes

Gun-filled nights curse the womb.
    Bullets, like rain,
Fall in monsoons.
A mama cries under the moon.

Don't die, little Johnny.
Hold on!
It's too soon!
Funeral Friday at noon.

Another point for
The keeper of doom.
Fed to the reaper
On a gun-powdered spoon.

Little Johnny
Age: Four
Gunshot wounds.

Meanwhile

A man-child hangs
In a cell.
Life's been a journey
Through hell.

Saw his mama in the courtroom,

JOURNEY JOHNSON

Bid her farewell.
Scrubbed his hands raw
Trying to cover the smell.

But it only drew blood
And made the teardrops swell.

Takes a gun to be a man.
Propaganda, they tell.
Now a million black minds
Find the truth in a cell.

We need help, Mr. President
But he shrugs, *Oh well.*
How long 'til genocide completion?
Only time will tell.

Jezebel

Jezebel turned tricks
    Like her mama turned tricks,
Like her mama before her turned tricks, too.

Had her singing Motown love songs
In the still of the night
To soothe her baby's blues.
Jezebel never heard a lullaby.

Why, I cry every time I think of the day
My Jezebel wrote me this song

It went like

Mary, don't you weep, now.
Mary, don't you weep, now.
Mary, don't you weep, now.
Hush

And a kiss left the drips
Of her tears on my lips,
And I could taste her demise in the salt.
And I knew it wasn't her fault.

She said she wouldn't be gone long
Said she wouldn't be gone.
Hindsight's 20/20,

JOURNEY JOHNSON

What she said was, *So long.*
When she wrote me this song.

Mary, don't you weep, now.
Mary, don't you weep, now.
Mary, don't you weep, now.
Hush

And she prayed the Lord my soul to keep,
But the tithes were too steep,
And she couldn't keep shoes on my feet.
Tried to bandage my cuts,
But the wounds ran too deep.

Mary, don't you weep, now.
Mary, don't you weep, now.
Mary, don't you weep, now.
Hush

You just stay right here in the closet
And don't make a peep.
Eviction notice on the door,
And you still gotta eat.
So, I'm a do what I'm a do,
But baby, please go to sleep.

And try to ignore
The moans and the grunts, and

Try not to smell
The pipes and the blunts, and

NECESSARY JOURNEY

Try not to hear
When he calls me a cunt, and

Try not to call it a 'trick'-
It's a stunt,
Cause it's a jungle out here,
And I'm on a hunt

So

Mary, don't you weep, now.
Mary, don't you weep, now,
Mary, don't you weep, now.
Hush

Door creeps open,
This motherfucker's smoking a blunt
Like this shit is a game.

And I'm kinda getting pissed
At this john called Coltrane,
Cause he's the type of nigga
Givin' good weed a bad name.

And I'm tryin' not to burn
In Jezebel's flames.
'Cause she's got nothin' to lose
And nothin' to gain.

And the thunder of her tears,

JOURNEY JOHNSON

Torrential like rain,
Roll like a whisper when he says
Bitch, call my name.

Battered and shattered
By the shadows of shame,
When she realized I saw it all,
No need to explain,
'Cause I'd never be the same.

And seeing in my future
The past from whence she came
Was a little too much
For Jezebel's brain.

Sanity crept quietly
One way out on the night train,
And I saw her in the morning,
Writing this song in the ice on the windowpane.

Mary, don't you weep, now.
Mary, don't you weep, now.
Mary, don't you weep, now.
Hush

And I pray the Lord my soul to keep
As she bundles me up
In last night's cum sheets.

And my little heart beats
To the strides that she glides

NECESSARY JOURNEY

Through the ice and the sleet.

And I'm clinging to life
On her sweet body heat.

And I swear I don't need
No shoes on my feet
If she could just find a way to keep me.
But...

Mary, don't you weep. Now.
Mary, don't you...

Mama, don't you weep!

Don't you lay me down
On this cold concrete
And don't you make me promises
That you can't keep

And don't you ever sell your soul
On some cum stained sheets
For me.

Mama, don't leave me.
There'll be no one to grieve me.
Don't need no shoes, please believe me,
Mama, don't leave!

But...

A kiss leaves the drips
Of her tears on my lips,
And I swallow the last breath of Jezebel's trip
In this hellhole

Singin'

Mary, don't you weep, now.
Mary, don't you weep, now.
Mary, don't you weep, now.
Hush

'Cause you got nothin' but time to hold onto
And...

Mary, don't you weep, now.

You got nothin' but space to belong to
And...

Mary, don't you weep, now.

You got nothin' to do but be strong, boo.

Mary, don't you weep now.
Hush

Jezebel wrote me this song.

Poet| Author

A native of the island of Hawaii, Journey is a daughter of Queen Lili'uokalani; she is a daughter to Harriet Tubman. Both of their lives can be found in the bold pain, rage, resiliency, and strength of her words.

    Her experience of spending twenty years on and off spoken word stages shines through in the rhythm of her writing style.

A recluse by nature, her work is quiet and calculating. She is an observer. She is an investigator. A reporter. A griot.

www.ingramcontent.com/pod-product-compliance
Lightning Source LLC
Chambersburg PA
CBHW020341010526
44119CB00048B/559

* 9 7 8 0 9 8 9 9 3 0 0 2 4 *